Five Steps to Marketing Success:

A Small Business Guide

The Best Marketing Guide for

Maximizing Business Success

Kiersten Kindred

Kiersten Kindred
Kindred Communications
kierstenkindred.com

Ordering Information:
Quantity sales. Special discounts are available on quantity purchases by corporations, associations, and others. For details, contact the publisher at the address above.
Orders by U.S. trade bookstores and wholesalers. Please visit kierstenkindred.com.

Printed in the United States of America

Five Steps To Marketing Success/ Kiersten Kindred—1st ed.

Credits:
Kiersten Kindred and Alexandra Alvarez – Cover design
Alexandra Alvarez – Illustration

ISBN-13: 978-1508826835
ISBN-10: 1508826838

Dedication

I dedicate this book to my mom, Betty, and my Auntie Margarite. They motivate me to be a better person and encourage me every day. I am forever grateful for their love and support. I feel so blessed to have them in my life, and I think I am the luckiest girl in the world to have such a loving, wonderful and understanding support system. This book would not have been possible if it were not for them inspiring me every day.

Thank you!

I also dedicate this book to my grandmother, Glinner. Although she is no longer here, I feel her spirit every day of my life, and without her lessons in life, I would not be the woman I am today.

To my family and friends, I greatly appreciate your support.

Love, Kiersten Kindred

~

Psalms 23.

Table of Contents:

Chapter One: Introduction

As a small business owner, you have to wear many hats in your company, and sometimes all the hats have to be worn at one time. Yes, this is a scary thought, but do not let matters fall through the cracks.

When talking to some business owners, I quickly realize they do not have a plan for marketing their company, and some may even confuse marketing and advertising as being the same activity, which is a big mistake.

Marketing is defined as, "The management process through which goods and services move from concept to the customer. It includes the coordination of four elements called the **4 P's** of marketing: (1) identification, selection and development of a **product**, (2) determination of its **price**, (3) selection of a distribution channel to reach the customer's **place**, and (4) development and implementation of a **promotional** strategy" ("BusinessDictionary.com," 2015).

Advertising is defined as, "The activity or profession of producing information for promoting the sale of commercial products or services" ("BusinessDictionary.com," 2015).

Advertising is a function of marketing. Marketing is about implementing a process to increase brand awareness and promotion. In my opinion, marketing is more important for business success, and this book will tell you why. In this book, you will learn how to establish and define your brand, craft your own comprehensive marketing plan, and gain the tools you need to efficiently tackle your marketing.

I know some of you may be thinking, why is marketing so important? Marketing is at the core of your brand. Good marketing will improve sales, increase exposure, implement steady and consistent progression within the company and much more. Marketing creates the image you communicate to your public, so the message has to be clear, concise and effective. How will you do this? Keep reading, and if you already happen to have a marketing agenda for your business, use this book as a guide to help refine your current brand.

Before you begin reading this book, it's important to understand that marketing your business may not be easy; sometimes you will not receive the outcome you are hoping to gain. Marketing is not a race; but it's a journey with rewards and challenges.

Marketing takes time to develop. You will have successes and setbacks. The key is to remember that you have to take your time developing a marketing strategy that best suites/serves your company. Many small business owners want to see marketing results in a month, and sometimes you might achieve that, but this success might only be temporary. Building your brand and audience are two of your most important business activities. Your audience comes from both potential customers and current customers. A strong, loyal customer base requires time to gain and retain. The marketing foundation you have built for your business determines your success. Think of the marketing foundation for your business like the foundation of a house. If the foundation is faulty, the house will always have problems. Your marketing strategy must be built on a strong foundation so that you will not have problems in the future. Your main goal for building a strong foundation should be two-fold: marketing to gain an audience and marketing to retain an audience. Having an audience to market to is the key to business growth and expansion.

This book will give you all the necessary tools needed to begin or refine your marketing efforts. Are you ready? Let's begin!

Chapter Two: Establish and Define Your Brand

Before you begin marketing to the public, your business must be established and defined.

What does it mean to establish your business? You have to build a strong foundation, which includes the following items:

- **Business Plan**
- **Legal and Financial Structure**
- **Location**

After you have these established, your business success will begin.

Establishing your business tells everyone that you are serious, and you are willing to do whatever it takes to ensure that your business will succeed. Properly establishing your business will help to encourage potential investors, clients, and customers to do business with you. If you do not have the proper foundation built in the beginning, you will pay for it later. Take the time to establish your business and do your research!

Once you have established your business, it is time to define your brand. We will discuss this in two parts, the components of your brand and the execution of your brand. Defining your brand is the most rewarding part of establishing your business. It allows you to be creative and take charge of your future. This includes the following:

Part I: The Components of Your Brand

       A. Crafting the perfect business or product name

       B. Logo

       C. Website

       D. Knowing your industry

       E. Company slogan

       F. Your secret weapon

Crafting the perfect business or product

Take the time to choose the perfect business name if you do not already have one. Your business name should be unique and simple. I always say less is best. A long name may be difficult for some customers to remember and spell. You want your brand name to be simple, clear and not already in use!

Logo

An impressive/memorable logo establishes the first impression customers have of your business. You may need a graphic designer to create your business logo, so consider hiring an expert. You might be the DIY (do-it-yourself) queen or king, but keep in mind that you want your business to look professional. You can brainstorm and design a logo to give to a graphic designer, that way you can save a little money and be involved in the creative process.

     Remember to design your logo with the consumer in mind. Ask yourself what you like as a consumer, what message would stay resonate in your mind, and whether you would buy from your own business? The logo is important, so spend a good amount of time on it.

Website

You can choose to design your own website or hire a professional web developer. Many do-it-yourself website builders will give you the professional look you want. Here are a few website builder sites that I personally use:

- Wix
- Wordpress
- GoDaddy (GoDaddy has an awesome website builder that allows you to easily create your own site in minutes, and their customer service is very helpful.)

Wix and Wordpress website builders offer free services, but you will not be able to have a free customized domain name. If you choose their free options, .wix or .wordpress will be placed after your site name. To gain all of the additional features they offer, I recommend that you pay for regular website usage on these sites.

DESIGNING YOUR OWN WEBSITE

If you plan to build your own website without the assistance of a website builder site, follow these **five** suggestions:

1) Choose a winning website domain name

The website name should be easy to remember and easy to

spell, in other words not difficult for your audience to understand. Check to see if the website name is already in use (Godaddy makes it easy to check).

The website name should be consistent with your business name. For example, my media firm is called, "Kindred Communications," the website name is kcfirm.com.

2) Register the name

Once you have decided a website name, register it with Godaddy.com. They have wonderful customer service and great prices!

Biz Tip: Always choose the *.com* option. Unless you are a nonprofit, you can choose *.org*. Choosing the *.com* option is important because everyone assumes a website name should have this designation. When developing a marketing strategy, always align your business image with the public's expectations.

3) Decide who you want to host your site

The hosting site is the connector between your domain name and the internet. Once you buy your domain name, purchasing a host service is like reserving your spot on the web, to make your site go live. A variety of websites provide hosting services. My suggestion is to purchase your domain name and hosting services from the same site. This helps you remain organized and makes it easier when contacting customer service for assistance.

Tip: Sometimes Godaddy will give you a discount for buying in bulk. Ask them about package options.

4) Create a website outline

Every business website should have basic components that includes: Homepage, What We do, Products and Services, Our Team or Who We Are, Work or Testimonials and Contact Us. Check out the details of each component below:

- *Homepage*: The homepage is the first page everyone will see when they are directed to your site. Be sure to captivate the audience within the first five-to-seven seconds.

- *What We Do*: This page will explain to the consumer what your company does and why.

- *Products and Services*: This page will have a list of all the products and services you provide. You might choose to put prices on this page depending on what business you are in.

- *Our Team or Who We Are*: Tell the world about the experts you have working in your company! This is the page where you boast about yourself and the people who work for you. It can be written in a satirical or serious manner. Put on your creative hat when writing this page.

- *Work or Testimonials*: Nowadays, people are visual and review-based. We want to see everything. As one commercial says, *"Show us the CarFax!"* Show the audience your work from previous jobs/clients to inspire trust in your company. If you have the kind of business that is not easily illustrated, show people your testimonials. When I am searching for a product or service, I look at the reviews and testimonials from previous consumers. The comments sometimes alter my judgment of a business and encourage me to conduct additional research on the company's background.

- *Contact Us*: Include your company's standard name, address, email, phone number, social media channels and fax number (if you have one).

5) Design your website

Once you have decided on a web name, registered the domain name, purchased the hosting and completed your outline, it is time to design your website. You can design your website with the help of the businesses listed in the website section above. I personally prefer Wordpress.com because it is the easiest option for those who do not know much about .HTML codes. In addition, Wordpress allows you to download handy plugins to your site. A plugin will allow the site builder to customize the site in important ways. It can increase options on a site, enhance users' experience, and provide additional software possibilities.

Tip: Search engines love multiple pages, content, pictures, and keywords; therefore, your website should contain more than one page.

In developing your website, keep the content and images clear and consistent. Your website will sometimes be the only impression your audience will have of you and your business; make it an attractive and professionally informative one. A website should not be created in just one day and considered to be a complete product. Take your time and do your research.

HIRING A FREELANCER FOR YOUR WEBSITE

If you decide to hire a freelancer to develop your site, visit these two valuable sites: www.freelancer.com and www.elance.com. When choosing a freelancer, request the following **six** items before contracting their services:

1) References: Request a minimum of three references from the freelancer. Call each reference and ask about his or her experience with the freelancer. Interview multiple candidates before you hire a freelance web developer.

2) Work portfolio: A proper work portfolio contains AT LEAST three samples of work. If you see only one work sample, it will be difficult to gauge their capabilities/skill level. When viewing a portfolio, it would be helpful to research terms a web developer should know about developing a site and quiz them on these. Test their knowledge before hiring them.

3) Pricing: Do not mislead the freelancer. Explain your budget to them, and ask if they would like to proceed. If your budget does not match what they typically charge, try to negotiate a better price. If you choose a freelancer, NEVER pay the entire invoice up front. Make a down payment on the site, and agree to pay the full amount after the site is complete. You do not want someone to take your money without doing the work.

4) Independent contractor agreement: If contracts are scary for you or you do not know how or where to begin with one, my favorite site is: www.rocketlawyer.com. They provide free legal documents and have a great system to help guide you in creating your own. The best feature of this website is that they will send the contract to the other party to sign if you provide the person's email. You will receive an email notification after the other party has signed the contract.

5) W-9: You will need them to fill out a W-9 for tax purposes. Go to irs.gov to get a free W9 document.

6) All contact forms from the freelancer, including their cell, website name and email. I once hired a freelancer, but I only had his email. This made me nervous because I was worried that he would leave me with unfinished work. Get all the information you can from your freelancer. Of course, you do not want to call their cellphone repeatedly but it is assuring to know that you can get in contact with someone and ask questions.

Knowing your industry

Would you let a person who did not know much about teeth fill your cavity? No.

Knowledge of your industry comes from your education or business background. Know your industry well before opening your business. Sound as knowledgeable as you can to gain the trust of others. Knowledge is power, and it will be your weapon against the competition.

Company slogan

Begin with your logo to create a tagline or slogan, both of which will take a lot of brainstorming. Try to make the slogan catchy and one that will be the first thought that comes to mind when looking for services in your industry. When I think of insurance, I think, *"Like a good neighbor, State Farm is there."* State Farm helped us remember their slogan by singing it to us, making funny commercials, and promoting them widely/extensively. When crafting a slogan, research other companies for motivation. Writing a slogan can be difficult, and you'll succeed if you invest the time.

Your Secret Weapon

Knowing your customer well is your secret weapon. To know your customer, you will have to learn what they like. Your goal should be to conduct research and gain useful knowledge of your customer; your business will prosper from this research.

Part II: Execution of Your Brand

The final steps in defining your brand includes: crafting an excellent mission statement, creating an elevator pitch, determining a target audience and defining your message.

Mission Statement

The mission statement of a business tells people exactly what to expect when investigating doing business with you. Include your mission statement on your website, brochures and key marketing materials. Use the theme of your business as your guide. Answer the 5 W's (who, what, when, where and why) when writing this statement.

Tell consumers who you are, what your business is, when you were established, where you are based and why you will provide the best service to them. The statement should be concise and compelling. A good mission statement should be 2-5 sentences. Keep the statement positive and uplifting to get people excited about your business.

Creating An Elevator Pitch

The elevator pitch will be your best friend, your wingman and your confidant. An elevator pitch is a brief overview of your business. This pitch will be used when talking about your business, with: potential investors, customers, family, friends, even the mailman. An effective pitch should inspire genuine interest in your company. When you are drafting an elevator pitch, imagine yourself at a networking event and someone asks you, "So, what does your company do?" Do you have a sentence or two already prepared that explains exactly what your business does? If not, let's craft one together. If you do have one, let's refine it!

The most important characteristic is the word length. The elevator pitch should not be too wordy, because it will seem as if you are unfocused place and that you do not have a focus. Plus, people's attention span does not last that long.

*Here are **five** questions each elevator pitch should answer:*

1) What is your business or product?

2) Who is your target audience?

3) Who is on your team?

4) Who is your competition?

5) How are you better than the competition?

Bonus: You can list your business accomplishments and accolades.

An effective pitch should be a speech which lasts under a minute and is well rehearsed. When you say your pitch, you should sound confident. If you sound unsure of what you are saying, people will notice.

Once you say your elevator pitch, give them a call-to-action. For example: "Now that you know a little bit about our business, feel free to participate in our monthly meet-up groups! You will learn more about how to build your nonprofit. Here is my card." When giving someone your card, do it with confidence. Make the person feel the importance of contacting and knowing you. It is all about your body language, which can make or break you.

Finding a Target Audience

A target audience is one of the most crucial elements in defining your brand. Your relationship with them will determine the success of your business. If you do not know your target audience, you need to learn who they are quickly.

To determine who your target audience is, investigate your industry, research the market and review your business.

Research your ideal consumer and gather data on the demographics and consumer patterns in your industry.

To get started, highlight or circle which demographic your business will target:

Gender: Female or Male

Age Group:

0-12

13-17

18-24

25-34

35-44

45-54

55-64

65+

What ethnicity is your target audience?

_____

_____

If animals are your market, which animals will benefit from your business?

_____

_____

Defining Your Message

What are you trying to accomplish with your business? What is your message to the public? How do you present this message to the public? Is your message well-received?

If you do not already have a message, you want to get one. Your message helps to expand your brand and keep you focused. The message should tell people what your company does and your plans for the future.

A well-written message will range anywhere between 50-100 words. It should quickly define who you are, what you are doing, and how you can help the customer. The message should spark the interest of your audience and enthrall and charm them. If you are not sure how to capture your audience's attention, ask yourself what you would want to hear from a business.

When you are trying to establish and define your brand, always have a goal in mind to get everyone excited about your business. Someone once told me, *"No one can sell you better than you can sell yourself..."* This quote has always stuck with me when I am trying to define my brand. I think to myself, I need to sell my brand quickly, get the audience excited, and speak clearly and concisely. Let the enthusiasm burst through your words when explaining why your business is an asset. Almost 90% of the time, people say no to a proposal, because they do not fully understand the concept, and they will not take the time to understand. This is where the message helps.

If you are having problems developing a clear message, listen to what your target audience wants and identify with them. For example: To encourage people to share videos, YouTube developed the simple slogan/message "Broadcast Yourself." This message is clear, you are not left with any questions and you can decide whether or not you want to use their service. Yes, this message is not 50-100 words, but it works for them. Typically, a message is longer than this YouTube example, so you can use it for different purposes and mediums; but if short works for your business, go with it.

A message is what you want your consumers to think about your business. To develop your message, visit the places you know your audience will be and gather research data. Places you can visit and listen to your audience include:

- Trade shows
- Internet message boards
- Marketing polls
- Informal gatherings in your industry
- Blogger websites in your industry. Bloggers tend to know more about what an audience wants because people come to them to receive non-sales content. Bloggers provide an informal environment where people feel safe and not pressured to make a purchase.

An excellent message is clear, simple, beneficial (to the target audience), consistent and easy to relate to. Practice your message until you are comfortable with it, marketing efforts require trial and error. Learn from your mistakes and keep it moving.

Chapter Three: Marketing Plan 101

In this chapter, you will learn to prepare, plan and draft an effective and successful marketing plan. We will review the following in this chapter:

- **Producing a marketing USP**
  - Three ways to craft a good marketing USP
- **Marketing Plan**
  - Business Assessment
  - Business Goals and Objectives Assessment
  - Analysis of Important Marketing Data (Customers, Competitors and Resources)
  - Name Your Price
  - Distribution Plan
  - Preparing a Realistic Sales Forecast and Budget
  - Marketing Budget
  - Communications
    - Website
  - Promotions
    - Social Media
    - Email Newsletters
    - Brochures
    - Flyers
    - Advertisement
    - Press
    - Events and Trade Shows
    - Networking
    - Blogging

- Company Gear
  - Action Plan

If followed correctly, this marketing plan will help you to increase your business. Let's begin!

PRODUCING A MARKETING USP

Before you begin drafting your marketing plan, what is your marketing USP?

Do you know what marketing USP is? (Circle one.)

Yes or No

In your own words define marketing USP:

_____

_____

_____

_____

Unique Selling Proposition (USP) is how your business is different or better than the competition. Combine your business USP with the concept of marketing and you have discovered how to market your business' individuality.

The marketing USP for my media firm, Kindred Communications, is built upon my mission statement, which is to generate the buzz for medium-sized businesses. Other firms may focus on strictly advertising a business, which may help them reach that target audience. Kindred Communications prides itself on providing services to clients that makes them feel like family. We embark on a hands-on approach to ensure each clients' goals are met, and this works for our target audience. Every firm has a marketing USP angle that works best for its target audience.

You may ask yourself, "Why do I need a marketing USP?" The USP lets your customer know why you, and not the competition, should be their provider. Your marketing USP should be at least one-to-two sentences and be quick and memorable. Here are **three** ways to craft an effective marketing USP:

1) Be an expert in your field. There are many ways to be seen as an expert in your field. You can try the following:

- Offer interviews to podcasts, radio shows or your local television station. To get on a show, contact the host or producer directly. You can find their contact information on their social media, website or blog. A podcast is the perfect media channel to reach your target audience, because it is niche driven.

- Develop your own blog. Building a blog audience is important; it is a way to tell people that you know what you are talking about without constantly trying to sell to them. For example, I named, Kindred Communications blog *The Marketing Recipe,* where I provide free expert advice about marketing. If you would like to learn more about it, here is the site name: kindredcommunications.wordpress.com.

- Attend speaking engagements. Begin speaking wherever you can. If you do not like to speak to a crowd by

yourself, volunteer to be on a panel of speakers at an event. If you do not consider yourself a speaker, then practice becoming a speaker. Work on your communication skills by taking a speaking class.

- Produce or write articles for the local newspaper. Offer your local newspaper free content in your field. Become best friends with the publisher and editor of the local newspaper and explain to them why it would be beneficial to them to have your content in their newspaper. Who does not like free, valuable content? This is an effective way to gain an audience and readership.

- Seminar Series. A seminar series is a way to educate people; when you become an educator, you become a respected authority in your field. Seminars offer an avenue to educate your potential consumers about the reason they need your service. Create a great series that will benefit people and that they can share with friends. Begin by drafting a PowerPoint presentation or an informational slideshow.

2) Do your research. How can you draft the perfect marketing USP if you have not done your homework? How has the competition set itself apart from other competitors? Conduct your own research by getting out there and diving into your market/industry. Approach the market or industry as if you are the consumer. Think about what makes your competition unique; what do they do to retain and increase their consumer base? Research the competition's website and their marketing channels. Gain an understanding of how they get their message out to people and what makes them so different than everyone else in the industry. Then learn your audience's preferences; determine what they consume and how they prefer to receive their information. This means understanding your audience demographic and conducting thorough research into how they like to receive advertisement. Conducting surveys or polls is the best way to learn this information. Visit your local library to gather more information about your target audience's demographics. You can view scholastic journals, which provide important/valuable/helpful information about various industries. Once you have completed your research, and feel that you know the trends in your industry, move to the next step – knowing your competition's weaknesses.

3) Understand your competition's weaknesses. Listening to the consumer is the best way to understand/discover your competition's weaknesses. You can view consumer's reviews on the competition by visiting the businesses' social media and open forum pages like Yelp, Google Reviews, Facebook and Twitter. People will voice their opinions. It is your job to know the consumers' grievances with your industry and know how you can improve the industry.

For example, business A has the following review on Google:

"I have shopped with this business for years, but their customer service is not very friendly. They provide great prices, but the customer service team deters me from shopping there."

Once you have read a review like this, it is your job to deliver better customer service than your competition. When you see that people do not like the customer service they are receiving from your competitor, you have an opportunity to provide better customer service, so people switch to your business.

When researching your competition's weaknesses, consider the following:

- How good is their product?
- Is the price range appropriate for the target audience? Can customers afford the competition's product?
- Describe the customer service experience.
- How quickly can people receive the service?
- Is the competition easy to find? (Location)
- Do people shop with other businesses in the industry? If so, list them.

Once you have answered these questions and followed the steps above, you will be better equipped to create your own marketing USP. *Here is my marketing USP equation:* The benefit to the consumer + a memorable phrase + authenticity + plausibility = your key to marketing USP success.

MARKETING PLAN:

Now that you have drafted your marketing USP, you can move onto your marketing plan.

Question: *Why make a marketing plan?*

_____

_____

_____

_____

Answer: *You have to know where you are going to know how to get there. A marketing plan will help you succeed. Your marketing plan is the map to your business growth.*

Conduct a business assessment.

<u>**Business Assessment Questions:**</u>

1) What is your business story?

_____

_____

_____

_____

2) What is your background?

_____

_____

_____

3) Your experience in the industry includes:

_____

_____

_____

4) What made you want to get into this industry?

_____

_____

_____

5) When did you enter this industry?

    Year: _____ | Month: _____

6) When did you start your company?

    Year: _____ | Month: _____

7) On a scale of 1-10, how well do you know your industry?

  1   2   3   4   5   6   7   8   9 10

8) Where did you open your business (location)?

_____

_____

_____

      Now that you have answered the personal assessment questions, begin crafting an easy-to-read marketing plan. A marketing plan does not need to be difficult or confusing. Make it easy; start with your business objectives, which can include the following: increasing sales and traffic, retaining customers and gaining visibility. What are your business goals and objectives? You can start by determining the following business goals and creating an objectives assessment.

Business Goals and Objectives Assessment:

1) Overall:

_____

_____

_____

_____

_____

2) Yearly:

_____

_____

_____

3) Monthly:

_____

_____

_____

4) Daily:

_____

_____

_____

5) What is your product or service?

_____

_____

Now that you have crafted your business goals and objectives, proceed with your marketing research.

What is the need for your product or service?

_____

_____

This is the place where your can conduct a SWOT.

S = Strengths

- What are the current strengths of your business?

_____

_____

_____

W= Weaknesses

- What does your company need to improve? Identify the industry knowledge you lack/need to develop.

_____

_____

_____

O= Opportunities

- Is there a potential avenue for your company to grow? What does your competition fail to do for the consumer that you can improve?

_____

_____

_____

_____

_____

_____

T= Threats

- **What does the competition do better that you cannot do or have failed to do? What do customers want from you? What are some future concerns for your business?**

_____

_____

_____

_____

To develop your SWOT, review the self-analysis of your business and conduct an in-depth customer analysis.

Who are your customers or target audience?

_____

_____

What is the game like now? (The industry)

For example, fifty years ago people received their news from a print newspaper, now the industry trend is for people to receive news electronically. If you are about to buy a print publication, you will want to know this information before investing in this business. Study your competition and do better. There is no need to imitate them. You should become your own brand and improve on the products and services you see them lacking.

When studying the competition analyze the following:

- Why might people choose the competition?
- Would it be difficult for you to go undercover to study the competition?
- How many competitors are in the industry?

After you have studied the competition, you are now ready to move into the most important part of the plan, the analysis of customers, competitors and resources.

Analysis of Important Marketing Data (Customers, Competitors and Resources)

Let's begin with the *customers.* When creating your marketing plan, ask these questions about your target audience:

1) Who are your customers? Who would you like to receive your product or service?

2) What do your customers like? When you determine your target audience, discover their preferences. What do they like? For example, when you are shopping for a book on Amazon, the company will tell you what people have also bought when buying this product, or the company will recommend another book with similar content. This is how you will want to think of your customer. When someone makes a purchase, what other products might interest them? Let's say I sale t-shirts, but to generate additional sales, I offer a sale on jeans because I know that the customer would like a complete outfit. Try to anticipate which products the customer might like while they are doing business with you. Would they like great customer service, a follow-up call, and coupons in the mail? Conduct research to determine what they would like. Be proactive!

3) When do your customers like to receive news/content/ads? Research when your target audience likes to receive their content and what time during the day or week they are more receptive to receiving a particular form of marketing. If you are posting tweets about your product at 3 a.m. and your target audience does not get to a computer until 9 a.m., this action could be unproductive. Read the studies that show when people are more likely to be on social media. This research can be used to determine delivery timelines for other aspects of marketing, such as: newsletters, mailers, advertisements and commercials.

4) Where are your customers located? Study the geographical location of your business. If you are selling an urban clothing line, your boutique should not be located in the suburbs. Keep in mind that your target audience should be able to reach you easily; consumers like to shop in their own community.

5) How will you reach your customers? Think about how you will reach your target audience. You can have a wonderful business, but if you do not have a plan about how you will reach people so they will hear about your business, wonderful does not matter. I believe in organic marketing, but you have to get out there and get the word out about your business. Hiring a street team and promotional assistants will increase your visibility and improve your marketing efforts.

6) Can your customers afford your product? Businesses sometimes neglect to do research about their business and their industry. It is important to learn what the consumer can afford. For example, my media firm helps small-and medium-sized businesses; and our most valuable selling point is that we work very closely with our clients. Our packages are priced according to our clientele and their needs.

7) What is your customers' income? Knowing your audience's income is important to help set your profit goals. This will require research. You can research the average income for your target audience by learning their careers. Another way to learn the average income of your target audience is to study the statistics of the geographic area. An example is when you are buying a house and you research the average income of people living in the area. Conduct the same kind of research for your business.

Now that you have distinguished the target audience for your business, let's study your *competitors.* Questions to ask when researching your competitors include:

- How do your competitors run their business?

- How did your competitors get to where you want to be?
- How do they get the word out?
- What is your competitor's price range?
- How good is your competitors' customer service?

To complete the analysis of your primary marketing data, you must ask yourself "what are my *resources?*" If you have a wonderful invention, but you cannot afford the products to put together the invention, how will you succeed? Will you need financial assistance? Think about your resources before you begin a venture. You would hate to begin something, get to the middle of it, and learn that you do not have the finances to carry out your plan. To get financial assistance, here are **three** resources to consider: apply for a loan at a financial institution, apply for a grant and consider crowdfunding.

Loan

Choose wisely when you are selecting a potential lender; your credit score could be adversely affected due to multiple inquiries or loan denials. Larger banks are known for turning down small businesses, so try to pick a lender that has a reputation for helping smaller businesses. Do not forget about credit unions!

Here are some items that you should be prepared to provide when applying for a loan:

- Your business and personal credit history

- A business plan (this is different from your marketing plan)
- Personal resume
- Financial projections and personal/business financial statements
- Business license or certification
- Loan application history
- Profit and Loss Statement (cash flow)
- Tax returns
- Driver license

Grant

When applying for a loan, simultaneously search for a grant. Everyone loves free money! Every business grant will have different requirements. Take your time when applying for grants and thoroughly answer each question.

Crowdfunding

If you decide to go the crowdfunding route, learn your options. Not sure what crowdfunding is? Crowdfunding allows a business to raise money by receiving funding from the community or the internet. Helpful crowdfunding sites are:

- Indiegogo
- RocketHub
- Kickstarter

View each site to determine how it can help your business. When you put your business on a crowdfunding site, tell your family and friends. Also, submit a press release to your local newspaper. Get the word out!

Name Your Price

Now that you have reviewed the most crucial part of your marketing plan, it is time to **name your price**. Think about how you will price your product or service and review your previous price ranges to determine how well they worked in the past.

When trying to determine a price, look at it as if you are working at a job. If a job pays you $40,000 a year, divide amount that into 12 months and that is $3,333, or is $833 a week, $167 a day, and $21 an hour. Now that you know how much you typically make when working for someone else, determine your pay rate. Break it down into small increments of time, and do not forget to add taxes and benefits. If you have a product you are trying to sell, analyze your costs (supplies, labor and other expenses).

Note: This is only a starting point for naming your prices. You can always adjust your prices according to what the market will bear and/or what you think is a fair price.

Distribution Plan

Once you have calculated your costs, determine how you will sell your product or service. **What is your distribution plan?** List three options below about how you plan to distribute your product or service:

_____

_____

_____

_____

_____

When devising a distribution plan, every business is different because the products are different. If you need an avenue to receive payment, check out the following options. Receive money anywhere with:

- PayPal
- Square

I personally use both, but I prefer PayPal. It is customer-and-business friendly. Put a PayPal button on your site and customers will click there to purchase your product or service. If someone does not want to pay through your site, you can also send them an invoice, through PayPal. The person will pay the invoice directly in the email through PayPal's trusted site. After they pay the invoice PayPal will automatically send that person a receipt, and it will add the payment to your PayPal account.

Preparing a Realistic Sales Forecast and Budget

Now that you know how you will receive your money, prepare a **realistic sales forecast and budget**. To do this, you need to examine the following:

- Outline your business (in 3-5 sentences).
- Set a budget goal that you would like to maintain.

- o Ideally, how much money would you like to spend monthly on your business?
  - Set a *realistic* goal of how much money you would like to make with your business (weekly, monthly and yearly).
  - Ask yourself what are potential changes to the market, competition and customers.
  - What problems might you encounter?
  - What are some potential operational changes that could incur?
  - List your KPI's (Key Performance Indicators).
  - What are your opportunities and threats?
  - Define your financial business cycle.

To finalize the plan, conclude it with a plan to review your monthly progress.

Marketing Budget

Creating a **marketing budget** is the next step. It always amazes me to find out how many businesses do not have a marketing budget plan. A business owner should plan to invest a good proportion of their money into marketing their business. Investing in marketing is the key to future growth and business success.

Question: Why do you need a marketing or advertising budget?

Answer: This form of budget will allow you to stick to your marketing plan and help you to avoid making costly, impulsive purchases or decisions.

Here is an example of a marketing and advertising budget plan:

1) Website.......... $1,000

2) Brochures (design and print).......... $300

3) Events and Trade Shows Yearly.......... $5,000

4) Sponsorships.......... $500

5) Gas.......... $50 (weekly)

6) Advertising.......... $1,000

7) Public Relations.......... $1,000

8) Memberships and Associations.......... $250

9) Search Engine Optimization (SEO).......... $500

10) Subscriptions.......... $250

11) Direct Marketing.......... $300

12) Internet Marketing.......... $500

13) Social Media.......... $200

14) Other.......... $500

Current Business Revenue	Marketing Budget (How much you are able to spend)	Business Expenses	Business Goal Profit
$55,000/year	$11,350	$20,000	$75,000

A monthly review of this marketing and advertising budget plan will help you remain focused. Business marketing budget plans will be different for each business because they make money from different avenues. For example, a clothing boutique might benefit the most at a trade show and less from radio advertisement placement, whereas a flower shop might realize the best Return of Investment (ROI) with radio ads. Decide which marketing or advertising avenue works best for your business and make a wise decision about where you should spend your money.

Some businesses make the mistake of only buying advertisements through local newspapers, magazines and radio stations. Then they question why they have not received any customer traffic. It is important to do the research before purchasing marketing products and spending your money in avenues that will not benefit your business. Observe what worked for the competition and if they already had a strong audience base before using that particular marketing avenue. Choose the best marketing avenue for your business to help you save money and make money in the long run. It is important not to go over your set budget, and if you do, make sure you gain a worthy return of investment.

Helpful Quote: "Study the unusually successful people you know, and you will find them imbued with enthusiasm for their work, which is contagious. Not only are they themselves excited about what they are doing, but they also get you excited." Paul W. Ivey.

Communications and Promotions

We are about to embark on my favorite part of marketing – **communications and promotions**! The fun part! In this section, we will cover the following items as a part of finishing your marketing plan: **website, social media, email newsletters, brochures, flyers, advertisement, press, events and trade shows, networking, blogging and company gear.**

Communications

Let's begin with **communications**. We touched on websites earlier in the book, but let's review it again.

Website

Your **website** should be your baby. Would you let just anyone babysit your baby? No. Be careful if you are not personally managing your website. Everything is a reflection of you, your brand and your business.

So far we have discussed the elements to include on your website, and creating a website yourself or hiring a freelancer. Let's review the text for your site. A lot of people focus primarily on the images for a site, but text matters, too. The text on your website should be creative and concise.

Readers do not like too many words. Business owners have a tendency to go on and on about what they are selling, but readers just want information that is straight to the point.

To add value to the site, you must maintain the interest of your audience. Providing unique content that readers cannot get from other places is an effective way to maintain customers' interest. For example, if you are a plumber, provide simple how-to videos on your website to help your viewers learn about the plumbing in their home. Viewers love this personal connection and will look forward to receiving more content like this in the future.

To ensure that your content is unique, you should organize it, properly. Think about how to be active in providing good content, how the content will make sense, the best way to tell the story, and how to communicate a concise and clear message.

Next, maintain customer interest in your website by consistently updating your site. Search engines love fresh content and images. The front page and the blog are the most important pages to update regularly.

When you update your site, tag every item properly. Your tags should be ones that people are searching regularly online. If you have a newspaper, your tags could be: [news], [city], [type of news], [news title].

While it is important to focus on tags, you should also focus on the headlines and images. Headlines should be short and keyword-friendly, while images should be crisp and clear. Too often, I see images on sites that are either too big or too small and unclear.

Page layout is another important aspect. Your page layout will say a lot about you. If your content is unfocused, this will communicate a similar message about your company. The same holds true for your content. If your content is vague it will suggest that you do not know that much about your industry. The navigation of your site is vital; organization and structure are imperative. Before you get ready to launch, test your site; click every link, headline, photography, and tab.

Install Google Analytics on your site. This tool is free and better than other analytic sites. My **six** personal favorite data displays that Google Analytics shows in its dashboard are:

1) Site Traffic: Here you can view how many people visit your site. The breakdown will include the day, the month, and the complete year. This data is helpful if you are trying to sell ad space on your site or if you are trying to attract investors.

2) Source: The source tab will show you how people find your site. It could be from another website or organically. This tool will tell you all you need to know.

3) Demographics: This tab will show you the site's demographics: gender, age and interest categories. Knowing this information will help you better engage with your target audience. Once you find out who is visiting your site you can better gage your content to keep them coming and encourage new users.

4) Audience Engagement: In this section, you can see where first-time users are visiting on your site and when they return to your site. You can view the economic impact of new vs. returning users.

5) Page Bounce Rates: This will tell you how long someone stays on your page.

6) Visitors' Location: Under the **Visitors** menu in the dashboard you will see the **Location** demographics for your visitors. Knowing where your visitors are located will help guide your choices.

While you are using Google Analytics, be sure to register your site with Google. Why is Google so important you ask? Because there are millions of websites, it is important that your website can be found on one of the world's most important search engines – Google, which offers a great set of tools to help get you on the internet map. 1) The first step is to submit your site at **www.google.co.uk/addurl/ (or Google search how to submit a website name)**. 2) Then submit a sitemap of your website to Google with their featured Webmaster tools. 3) After you register your site with Google, you can move on to other search engines such as Yahoo: https://search.yahoo.com/info/submit. 4) Register your site with at least three search engines.

Promotions

Promote your website by: 1) beginning with who you know. Business success depends on who you know. Tell everybody – family, friends and associates about your business. Encourage people to spread the word about your site and what makes your site unique. 2) After you tell the people you know about your site, tell the world! Display your site on a) social media channels, b) in your email newsletters and c) post to outside sources.

Social Media

Now that your website is finished, let's take a deeper look at **social media**. Before reviewing your social media channels, make sure **not to mix your personal social media pages with your business social media pages; they are different. Keep your business pages on a professional level and keep your personal views to yourself.** To understand the importance of social media, view the statistics of each channel, at Statista.com, which tracks most popular social media sites in the United States in August 2015. This data is based on market share of visits.

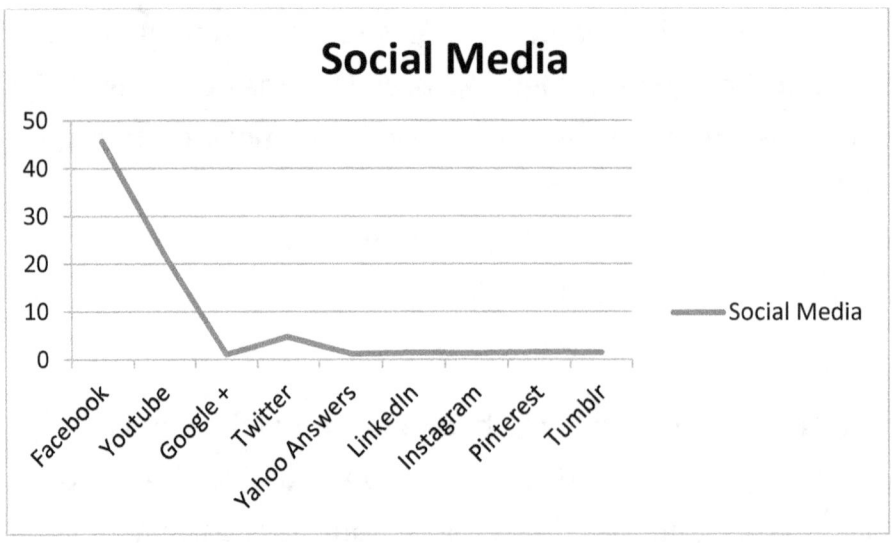

Currently, every data research site ranks Facebook as number one in number of users. The following chart offers/highlights different yet similar data findings to help you compare and gain a better understanding of social media.

Wix.com highlights the best social media channels according to the number of users.

Social Media Data Breakdown (March 2014)

- Facebook: used by 1.23 billion users
- Twitter: 650 million users
- Google Plus: 550 million users
- LinkedIn: 280 million users
- Pinterest: 70 million users
- Instagram: 150 million users

Now that you have a better understanding of how many people use social media and which are the best options for your business, let's review how to use social media to benefit your business.

Social media is used as a promotional tool, but don't abuse it by constantly pitching and selling to your audience. Have conversations, teach, and share something interesting with your audience. Throughout the day, post to each of the following social media channels in this manner:

- Facebook: 3-4/daily
- Twitter: 4-5/daily
- Instagram: 1-2/daily
- Periscope: 1/daily
- Google Plus: 2-3/daily and join a new circle once a week
- LinkedIn: 2-3/daily
- Pinterest: 1/daily
- YouTube: 1-2 new videos a week

You might ask why you have to post to social media so much. The key is to be visible to the customer. Social media has become so important in recent years that you cannot survive without it. Practice posting daily. If you are unable to do this, get an online dashboard, such as Hootsuite or Tweetdeck, that will automatically post for you.

It's important to be patient with social media. If you get frustrated with it or impatient with the results, do not abandon your social media; it takes time to see growth. In recent years, people have begun to buy followers, but this is a high risk. Social media channels can suspend your account and delete both your real and fake followers. Be genuine, and build your social media yourself. Here are my top **five** tips for maximizing social media:

1) Your social media channels should be filled with keywords, links, pictures, videos and compelling content.

2) Engage with your current customers and potential customers.

3) Know your customer and know what they like.

4) Keep your hashtags to a minimum. #Yes #I #Said #It!

5) Measure your social media progress. Learn what works and what does not work.

Social media can be your best friend and your worst enemy. It can be a double-edged sword. While you *hope* for happy customers to engage with, you can also get angry customers leaving unflattering comments on your page. Always respond in a professional manner, and let other customers see that you genuinely care about your customers and you listen. Keep in mind that customer service carries over to social media, as well.

To help measure and track your social media growth, complete the questionnaire below:

1) What are your social media channels?

_____

_____

_____

_____

2) Which social media do you spend the most time on and why?

_____

_____

_____

_____

3) How many followers do you have on each social media channel (beginning with the top six)?

- Facebook likes: _____

- Twitter followers: _____

- Google Plus views: _____

- Instagram followers: _____

- LinkedIn connections: _____

- YouTube subscribers: _____

4) Are you currently active on the social media channel where most of your target market is located?

_____

_____

_____

_____

5) How do you currently post your content? (What is your theme?)

_____

_____

_____

_____

6) How often do you currently post to each social media channel?

_____

_____

_____

_____

7) Is your presence felt on social media? Are you engaging with your followers?

_____

_____

_____

_____

8) Do you have the time to manage your own social media? If not, why?

_____

_____

_____

_____

Social media is important to a business. As a business owner, you should utilize this marketing channel to help you increase awareness of your business and to grow. Do not be afraid of social media. It is a trial and error platform. Let the web be your playground and play all day.

Email Newsletters

If you have never sent an **e-newsletter** to your customers or potential customers, the time has come! Don't miss another big opportunity. Email newsletters keep you in contact with your customers, builds relationships, promotes your business, and, most of all, help communicate quick updates about your business activities. Think about it. How many times a week do you check your email? I check my email at least 30 times a day; this would be an effective avenue for people to reach me as a consumer. Take this into consideration and build your own email newsletter campaign.

You can pay for someone to create and send an email newsletter or you can be a DIY king or queen and do it yourself! If you decide to do it yourself, here are helpful sites that will help you build a winning email newsletter campaign.

My favorite email newsletter campaign sites are:

1) Constant Contact: They have WONDERFUL customer service!

2) Mail Chimp: Free for up to 2,000 subscribers! Ding, ding, ding…a small businesses' best friend!

3) Campaign Monitor: They offer an efficient way to organize your content.

The key to building a unique and engaging email newsletter is to provide valuable content. Your content should be information that people cannot get from another outlet.

In your newsletter, always stay on topic. If you sell houses, don't tell your audience how to make a *mean* margarita – tell them the easiest way to apply for a house loan. Stay on topic, and keep it short and sweet. Keep in mind that most people have a short attention span. We do not want to read a two-page newsletter.

A newsletter should portray a specific tone which is communicated in the subject line. Your subject line should be captivating and interesting. It is the first thing customers see and it lets them know if the email will be engaging. Do not use a subject line such as "Sally's Cupcakes: January Newsletter." Your subject line should make people want to read your content, visit your site and shop with you. The subject line could be, "Exclusive Interview with Chef Gordon Ramsay!" Entice your audience to open the email.

Once a customer opens your email, they should discover a message that should be easy on the eyes, and filled with interesting content, videos and pictures – all presented in an organized manner. Keep this information simple and clean, because customers grow frustrated when they have to read through scattered information.

An effective newsletter should include the following:

- **Subject:** An excellent subject line is concise and captivating.
- **Brief news items and updates about your company:** Keep this section SHORT! Share updates about your company that customers find interesting. Customers are not interested in your email system update; rather, tell them how you hired a new CEO and how this new person will help the consumer.
- **Leading stories:** This section should be interesting. Think about interesting company or industry stories that people may not know. Your content should be conversational. This entire section does not need to be in your newsletter. Users can click on a link to see the full article on your site if they want to read more. This section can also be taken from your blog.
- **Exclusive items (coupons, interviews and tips):** When thinking of exclusive items to include in the newsletter, think about what you are willing to give up. Do not give too much free advice; you still want the consumer to utilize your services. Give only enough information to encourage the customer to learn enough about your business to peak their interest in becoming a

customer. People say *no* to things they do not understand, but if they understand the importance of your product or service, they will better understanding about why they need to utilize it.

- **A message from the CEO or owner:** A message from you, the business owner, should be 1-2 sentences. In this section, include a thank you and tell your customers information you are eager to reveal. This section is your opportunity to build a relationship with your audience, so make it count!

- **At least 1-2 photographs:** Your photos should be related to your business. The reader should be able to view the photo no matter which channel they use to view your email.

- **A video:** You do not have to be a video editor to create an interesting video for your newsletter. The video can be a behind-the-scenes look at your company, interviews, or a quick how-to instructional piece. Buy an inexpensive, little camcorder to record videos, and you can edit them with a free video editor. If you have a smart phone, there is an application that will allow you to edit your video. Keep in mind that your video should be short and clean. Your customers do not want to view a video that is out of focus or too loud – keep your audience in mind.

Compared to other marketing channels, a newsletter is an effective, inexpensive avenue that offers a high ROI. Do not forget to send a weekly newsletter to remain current with your customers. Newsletters are inexpensive marketing tools, but sometimes you need to spend a little money to produce a quality product that can be used to attract customers and help spread the word about your business. A **business brochure** will achieve this goal**.**

Brochures

A brochure is a useful tool because you cannot be everywhere at once but your brochure can. While you are attending an event, your brochure can be at the local coffee shop attracting customers.

An effective brochure should compel people with its use of engaging writing and explain to your potential customer the benefits they will receive from doing business with you. Brochures boost sales by helping people understand why they *need* your business and by encouraging them to visit your site to learn more. Think of a brochure as a teaching lesson. When you are learning something, you want to know the **5 W's: Who, What, When, Where** and **Why.**

Here is a sample of a tri-fold brochure format:

Front:

The front of your brochure should display/contain a compelling graphic that appropriately represents your business. It should include your business logo, name, website and an attention-getting title.

Inside:

The **first page** should explain your business. This is the **Who, What and When** aspect, which tells what your business is, when you opened for business, and what it is that you do. Paraphrase the *About Us* page from your website, which should be about a paragraph each, one for the **Who** and one for the **What**. Include a photograph of your business. Do not confuse people with too much text, but include enough explanation so people will understand your business.

The middle page should contain the lesson, which explains **Why** customers need your business and **How** you can help. The middle page is the most important! Your wording should be persuasive. Use bullet points to highlight why people need your business. Keep this section clear and concise. Too much text will appear cluttered and people will not take the time to read it. Remember this section should include the following: bold titles and subtitles, proper spacing and legible font. Do not forget to offer some eye candy in this section, too. Include graphics and photos to make your point about why people *need* your business.

The right side of your brochure should encourage a call-to-action (tell customers what you want them to do). A call-to-action includes be the following: directions, including a map to your business, how to access your website, and a coupon or a form for the customer to complete. You have to tell your customer what you want them to do, otherwise, how will they know the best way to use your services?

This following section addresses **Where.**

The outside of the brochure might include pictures and your best contact information.

Check the prices of various copy shops because some might offer a discount based on the quantity you are having printed. Begin with 100 copies. Do not go overboard with printing unless you have a guaranteed audience. Save your money and spend it wisely.

Place your brochures where they will reach your target audience or leave them for potential investors. Determine which places are most important when distributing your brochure and give them a quality paper brochure. Invest! Before you leave your brochure at a location, ask the owner's permission to leave your brochure. Many locations will throw away paper that has not been approved. If you want to give the location an incentive for holding your brochure, you can give them a percentage off your product or service for every referral received by that location. Encourage people to spread the word about your business! Keep your brochure simple and clear. Entice your audience to want more.

Flyers

Flyers are another important aspect of your marketing campaign. Flyers are a quick way to give information about your business and reach a larger audience. Your flyer should include the following key elements: your company's name, a good headline, your logo, a call-to-action, photo, important bullet points about your business (what you do, how you can help, and the benefit to the customer), and contact information. If you have a promotion, include it in big, bold letters.

Producing a flyer will probably be the easiest task in your marketing campaign, but be aware because there is more room for error here. In the past, I have seen posted flyers containing various errors. Too often, people create flyers in an hour or two, and they fail to proofread and check the information it contains. Take your time and check everything on your flyer. When I create a flyer, I write or draw it on paper first. I'm old-fashioned. Then I create it on the computer.

Your flyer should include the following elements, which will distinguish your company from the competition: bold lettering, different fonts, an enticing headline, a bold color of paper, graphics, a separation of sections with boxes and designed lines.

Be aware of:

- Wordiness
- Small font
- Misspellings
- Light-colored font
- Not proofreading
- Too many technical terms

Advertisement

Your next marketing initiative should be **advertising,** which effort is the trickiest and most expensive. People confuse ad space as only a way to get customers directly, but advertising is mainly about brand awareness. If you happen to get some customers in the process, it is a bonus. I have worked with some business owners who put ALL their money into ad space and wonder why customers fail to materialize. Ad space is not a guarantee of success. Simply putting out ads or content hoping that someone will remember to use your business is not enough.

When shopping for advertisement space, think about how you personally like to receive ads, how often you pay attention to ad spaces, and if those ad spaces inspire you to do business with that particular business.

For example, I was driving to work and saw the billboard for 93.7 The Beat promoting The Breakfast Club morning show. When I saw the billboard, I thought about turning on my radio to see if I could catch Charlamagne's *Donkey of the Day*. Listening to my radio was not on my mind, but as soon as I saw the billboard I thought, *"Hey, let me tune in as I head to work."* The billboard message reached my subconscious and succeeded. I personally like to receive my ads via television commercials, billboards or on a website (especially a website banner).

Name three ways you like to receive your ads?

1) _____

2) _____

3) _____

Now that you have considered the three ways you like to receive advertising, think about the most effective way to reach your audience. Reference your list above.

Questions to ask when deciding where to buy ad space:

Q: **Who is my target audience?**

A: _____

Q: **Where is my target audience located?**

A: _____

Q: **What is my advertising budget?**

A: _____

Q: **When is the best time to reach my target audience?**

A: _____

Q: **In which two places would I like to begin advertising?**

A: _____

Begin with only two locations for advertising placement because you want to remain within your marketing budget. First, determine what works then proceed with other advertising avenues. Conduct research and be observant. Study where your competition is advertising, and listen to how people respond to their ads. Other factors to consider when deciding where an ad would be well received are: how many people will view this ad (get the numbers), how big will the ad space be, and do the service providers have a package deal and/or perks for your business?

When you are buying ad space from various places, price shop. If you rush when buying ad space, it could cost you money. Take your time and make cost-effective choices.

Press

Getting **press,** which is another challenging aspect of marketing, is your next step. It is difficult to get free press – especially if you do not have a press contact.

Obtaining press for your business is all about who you know and networking. You can hire a public relations firm to get media attention for your business, or you can do it yourself.

Organization and structure is imperative. First, conduct research on the media channels you would like to cover your business, and add their contacts to an Excel spreadsheet. Organizing all the media's numbers and emails in one place will help you determine who you want to contact first and help you track who you have already contacted.

Second, draft a standard email or press release explaining what you are trying to have covered and why they should cover it. This step is the most important. When I was a reporter and columnist for a local newspaper in Texas, I received countless emails from businesses, nonprofits, local residents, and politicians trying to get their story published in the newspaper. The most impressive emails and press releases were the ones that:

1) **Told a story.** A lot of media outlets covered a Domino's Pizza Store that delivered pizza every day to a woman. When she skipped a couple of days, the employees decided to call 911 to see if she needed medical help. Their concern saved her life.

2) Tugged at my heart. I covered a story about a local nonprofit that was helping people learn how to read. I thought readers would like this story because they may have known someone who could not read and they could refer them to the nonprofit mentioned in the story. It was touching to me that so many people volunteered to help others learn a fundamental skill.

3) Helped the community. A local insurance firm held a toy drive every year, and the members of the community loved it because those who could not afford toys for their children were able to give their children Christmas gifts.

4) Something new and innovative. If you have a new technology or a new way of doing things effectively, pitch the story to a reporter, and they are likely to cover it.

5) Strange stories. If you are a business person, simply get your name out in the public. Sometimes you can begin with anyway possible, just to establish a relationship with a reporter. I remember a local businessman who told me he loved seeing new puppies play with toy balls, and this image inspired him to open his own doggie daycare.

6) Add date and time. I covered stories that had a specific date and time stated on the press release or request form, first because I knew that the subject matter had a deadline. We called these articles "time sensitive."

Be interesting and creative with every story that you are pitching to the media. Once you have submitted your story to a reporter, follow-up with a friendly email and a call the next week. Keep in mind that there is a thin line between a standard follow-up and being a pest. Do not bug them. They receive hundreds of emails a day. The key is to find a happy medium to keep your business on their minds.

Events and trade shows

Events and trade shows are important to your marketing efforts because they give you exposure and boost your brand awareness, while hopefully making some sales. Do not simply buy a booth for every event or trade show. Do your research. When trying to decide which events or trade shows to attend. Ask the event manager or organizer the **eleven** following questions:

1) What is the show about?

2) How many years have you held this event or trade show?

3) Where is your organization going to hold the event?

4) Who usually attends the event or who are you targeting to attend the event? The answer to this question should give you the customer demographics.

5) When is the event?

6) What is included in the event package? Sometimes, if you buy a table at an event, the organizer will include you in their newsletters and on their social media outlets, and may even add you as a sponsor. Ask about their potential perks!

7) <u>MOST IMPORTANT:</u> How many people are projected to attend the event? Ask about the event's projected numbers and the RSVP contact list.

8) How big will my table space be? May I speak or make announcements at the event?

9) How are you promoting the event?

10) What are the various packages you offer to businesses? This is how you gain an understanding of the various packages offered by the event planners and which would be the best option to expand your business. For example, you may not want to buy a table, but you still want your presence felt at the event. Your best option is to get a placement in the goody bags distributed to the attendees. (Get this information via email).

11) How often are you promoting this event?

These are only a few of the questions to get you started when inquiring about events, but you can always ask for more information. Get everything in writing, because you do not want people to retract what they told you via phone.

Networking

As a small business owner, you will thrive off of **networking.** Networking will be a significant part of your business because one of the most important marketing tools is word-of-mouth. Sometimes, a business can survive solely on word-of-mouth. Do not neglect this outlet of communication with the public. It is crucial to build relationships.

Now, with virtually everything located online, it is easier for you to connect with people all over the world. Sometimes I simply send an email and say I would like to work together on a small project to maximize our resources. This is great way to build relationships because you never know when that may grow into a mutually beneficial alliance. It is all about building partnerships and possible partnerships everywhere.

You must have a plan when networking in person. Have a strategy about *when, where and how* you will network. If you have an 8-5 job, it can be difficult to network for your business AND work at your day job. Of course, you want to focus on your business to be your full-time job one day, so you must make wise decisions to make your dream a reality. This means attending only important networking events that will give you the most exposure. A lot of times networking events are expensive, so those events must be planned strategically to fit your marketing budget. Network anytime possible, but avoid going overboard. Many times, business owners focus too much on networking and building relationships instead of focusing on their business and gaining clients.

You can network everywhere. To begin networking, here are some great places to consider:

- Look on **Eventbrite.com** to see where networking events are happening in your city. Go to the search engine box and search for keywords like *networking, small business, and marketing*. Events on this site have to be searched carefully because anyone can advertise an event. Make sure to use wise judgment when selecting networking events. Determine if attending a particular event will be worth your time and money. Your time is more valuable than your money because you will never get your time back.

- Visit **Yelp** to see what upcoming events are related to your business and which ones would be the most beneficial to attend.

- **Research websites that hold networking events or post where other networking events are held.** Once you have located at least three websites, join their mailing list and be on the lookout for their next event. If they send too many emails, you can remove yourself from the list and add it to your junk email account. A junk email account is an email address used as a junk email recipient. Check this email address once a week.

- **Join community groups.**

- **Become a member of an organization.** In your professional field if you want to increase your chances of networking in this organization, take a leadership role. When taking a leadership role, make sure that it will not take ALL of your time. I accepted a leadership role within a professional organization, and it took all my time. Between going to weekly events, having to network, and planning events, I had limited time to dedicate to my business. Always be careful when choosing a leadership role. Confirm the time it will take from you before you assume the role.

▪ **Become a member of the Chamber of Commerce**. Being a member of the Chamber of Commerce is *very* important no matter what industry you are in because it provides opportunities for your business. You will meet people from a variety of industries and backgrounds. Even if you cannot determine how they might be beneficial to your business, you never know when you may need their expertise in the future. The Chamber of Commerce gives you a direct connection to the city. It is important to know what is happening in your city and how you might be able to help. You might even be able to form a partnership or provide a service for a new development in your city. Take risks!

▪ **Attend networking events, special interest groups and professional industry meetings.**

▪ **Research Google Hangouts and Twitter Chats**. Businesses will sometimes host a group discussion on a Google Hangout or begin a Twitter Chat using a hashtag. This is a great way to meet people from all over the world. Once you build your audience, you can start your own Google Hangout or Twitter Chat. These discussion groups are perfect for networking and connecting people within your industry. An added bonus to this activity is that you will be regarded as the expert in your industry by hosting these events and by leading the conversations.

▪ **Enroll in a business class or workshop.** I have met a lot of entrepreneurs in business classes and workshops. Everyone is open to networking and learning. In the future, you may be able to exchange services and help one another. Small business owners have to collaborate.

■ **Attend local and national conferences**. I love attending national conferences because I meet like-minded people all in one location. Attending at least one important conference a year. Conferences are expensive, especially if they are well attended. In my opinion, networking at conferences is the easiest form of networking because people usually attend these events alone, which allows you to make connections with them. It is more difficult to network with people when they come with people they know. I always feel more comfortable when I am networking one-on-one, which makes it easier to approach people and begin a conversation. Go to conferences with the intention of learning, networking, and selling.

Become comfortable with your networking skills. If you do not know how to network properly, here are **four networking tips:**

1) "I'm going to let you finish, but..." **Do not interrupt people**. If the person that you want to talk to is talking to someone else, do not interrupt their conversation. Wait and introduce yourself when they finish talking.

2) **First impressions are everything**. Make them count! Be on point with your appearance, which is part of your brand. Your clothes should be appealing, and your appearance must be polished. It is essential for your body and breath to smell good. Talking to someone with bad breath is off putting.

3) **Offer a handshake, make eye contact and say your name with confidence**. If you are nervous about meeting people, practice in the mirror or take a class.

4) **"Enough about me. Tell me a little about you." Get to know the person you are speaking with. Do not monopolize the conversation.** Ask questions and indulge in follow-up questions. Talking about yourself without asking a question suggests that you do not care. If you do not get to know who you are talking with, then you will not know how you can possibly collaborate with them in the future.

Ask the following questions:

- Tell me about what you do?
- Do you enjoy your field?
- What does your job or business entail (details)?
- How and when did you get started?
- What do you like most about your job or company?
- How is your industry going? What is the current state of your industry?
- Where do you see your industry going in the future?
- Are you affiliated with any other organizations?
- Are you originally from (city)?

To expand your network, remember questions that you would like to ask people, that way there will not be any awkward silent moments. You can enhance the conversation with relevant questions. When you are networking remember the following:

1) Keep it G-rated. When you are in a professional networking environment, be mindful of your word choices. Do not curse.

2) Exchange business cards before you leave. Always bring at least 30 business cards to each networking event.

3) Send a follow-up email. Tell them it was a pleasure to meet them and that you look forward to keeping in contact. Direct them to your website and encourage them to follow you on social media.

Sometimes networking is the only effective marketing tool your business has. Find a balance between attending networking events and effectively working on your business.

Blogging

If you are not sure why a blog is important to your business, study the "**Seven** Reasons to Begin a Blog" list below:

1) Increase brand awareness. The more promotional content you have out in the viral universe, the more people will know about you and the services or products you offer. A blog will generate a new audience base for you that might lead to potential clients.

2) Take the crown. Provide unique content that people cannot get from other sources. Give people new information that will help them trust you and view you as a leader in the industry.

3) Improve SEO

Question: What exactly is SEO?

Answer: Search Engine Optimization (SEO) is the practice of optimizing a site internally and externally to increase the site's number of viewers from search engines and to help improve the rankings on these engines.

If you are writing with SEO in mind, your blog will be successful. Write with the goal of creating excellent content, adding compelling photographs, having a unique name for each title and adding often searched keywords. Visit Google Keyword Planner to determine the best keywords. Here is the site domain: https://adwords.google.com/KeywordPlanner (this is a powerful tool!)

4) Another outlet to sell. Your blog should not be solely about selling, but it *can* be a unique channel to tell people about your product or service. Don't tell them too often. I have seen many business blogs fail because they are constantly trying to sell to the reader. Your blog should help readers and provide interesting content – not another place where you pitch to them. Every once in a while you can mention your product or service, but do not do it constantly.

5) Helps to build a relationship with your customers.
People view a blog as a leisure activity, not a shopping outlet.
Connect with your audience here, ask questions, provide
answers, and commentary. Let people know there is an
informed person on the other side of the internet connection.

6) Drive the audience to your website. Telling people
about your website can be difficult, but your blog can be
another place where you promote your website. Create a post
every month about something new on your website, and
encourage people to visit it.

7) Open new doors for your business. This statement
may be confusing, but think about it. People attend hundreds of
blogging conferences. Because you blog now, you can attend
these conferences and promote your business.

Produce a blog at least one-to-three times a week. You
have a better chance of organically building awareness about
your business with the more content you feed to the web.

If you do not want to pay for a business blog, here are some
important sites that offer a free space to host your blog:

- Wordpress.com
- Blogger.com
- Tumblr.com
- Weebly.com
- Wix.com
- Blog.com

Company Gear

Company gear provides another way to promote your business. Your company gear should be simple and eye-catching.

Attractive and easy company gear can include:

- Shirts
- Caps
- Socks
- Calendars
- Key chains
- Magnetic stickers
- Coffee cups
- Pens
- Fans
- Post-it notes (with your logo)
- Pencils
- Small bags

Company gear helps increase brand awareness without having to constantly tell people about your business. To begin your marketing efforts using your company's gear pick one or two of the options listed above. Begin with shirts and key chains, because those are the most cost effective and could provide a high ROI.

Action Plan

The **action plan** is the last step in your marketing plan. How will you implement everything you have written down and planned?

Implementing your action plan will take trial and error. Once you sell something, evaluate the process that lead up to that sell, and determine what worked and what did not work.

Every time I wanted to give up on something, my mom told the story about the cleaning product Formula 409. Do you use this cleaning product? Great stuff! Formula 409 was invented by two young Detroit scientists who were trying to create a cleaning solution. They tried 409 times before they found the perfect formula; thus, the name 409.

Can you imagine trying something 409 times? Most people would have called it quits after trial No. 50, but the scientists continued because they believed in themselves and their product. You will need to have the same perseverance and commitment for your business to succeed. Few things in life that are worth having are ever easy, but what is worth having is worth working for – keep trying and never give up!

Chapter Four: Marketing Kit

Now that you have completed your marketing plan, let's move on to your **marketing kit,** which will be sent to the media, potential investors and clients. You need a marketing kit because it will inform people about what you are doing and what you have done in the past.

Question: Where do I distribute my marketing kit?

Answer: Distribute your marketing kit to whomever requests it and to media outlets.

The following items should be included in your kit: *business cards, a flyer or brochure, referral cards, a press release, your media kit and a list of your social media channels.* Your kit can be both in a physical and digital form.

Let's begin by building your marketing kit:

1) Business Card: Having a business card is important because it helps give you publicity. The key elements to every business card are: *company name, your name, email and contact number, website and company logo.* Use eye-catching colors and fonts that are easy on the eyes. Your business card is the first impression someone has of you and your business, so make it memorable.

If you cannot find a store to produce and print your business card, try the site I use for all my printing materials:

vistaprint.com; this site that has wonderful pre-made templates and helpful customer service.

2) Flyer and/or Brochure: Include a flyer or brochure in your marketing kit to help inform people about your business. Include 1-3 flyers in your marketing kit.

3) Referral Card: Give people an incentive for referring your business.

4) A Media Kit: A media kit gives people a quick overview of your business and enables them to understand what you are trying to achieve. Your media kit can be public or private. If it includes your price list, I would suggest making it private. A media kit can also help you get press quickly, because your information is only an email away.

A sample media kit includes:

- Your company logo and graphics
- Information about your company
- What your company does
- The process of your business (how all the magic happens in your business)
- Your statistics and numbers (if applicable)
- Pricing
- Testimonials
- CEO/ owner biography
- Contact Information

5) List of social media accounts: Include a list of social media accounts and their statistics. List the major business social media accounts that include: Facebook, Twitter, YouTube, Google Plus, and LinkedIn.

6) Press Release: The most important component of a marketing kit is a press release. A press release is great for any industry because it offers information about an event, a major news story or new aspects of your company.

Questions to ask yourself when writing a press release:

- What is the subject or purpose of my press release?
- Is the event or information in the press release newsworthy?
- What am I hoping to gain from a press release?
- Should I distribute this press release locally or nationally?
- How urgent is this press release?
- Will the message in my press release be over a page long?
- Is the message within my press release clear and concise?

Have you ever drafted a press release? If not, we have provided instructions about how to create the perfect press release, along with a fill-in form of a press release so you can create your own.

How to Create the Perfect Press Release

First, start with a <u>header.</u> The header is at the top left corner of the release and will have your contact information. *For example:*

FOR IMMEDIATE RELEASE
Date
MEDIA CONTACT: Kiersten Kindred
Company Name
Phone Number
Email

After you have completed the header, move onto the **<u>subject line,</u>** which subject line should be interesting and captivating.

Your next section is the **<u>opening section</u>** of the press release. In this section, briefly discuss what the press release is about, and offer a teaser. This section should only be about 1-2 sentences long because you want to quickly gain the attention of whoever is reading it. When developing this section, think of novel, creative words to entice your reader to read more.

The next step is the **<u>body</u>** of the release. Since this is the focus of the release, your reader should be able to understand everything you are trying to convey from reading this section. This section should be a full paragraph (3-5 sentences). Give your reader the 5 W's and include a personal quote.

<u>Boilerplate</u> comes next. What is a boilerplate? I took professional development classes and studied marketing and had never heard of this term until I got my first professional job after college. Google describes boilerplate as a section that goes in every press release you send out, and it will tell the reader about your business. It should be about 3-5 sentences length. Use your mission statement as a reference. Be sure to include your company website here and a business address if you have one.

Lastly, include **three centered pounds signs** (# # #) to the bottom of the press release to let the reader know they have reached the end.

Sample Press Release Form:

FOR IMMEDIATE RELEASE
(Date)
MEDIA CONTACT: _____
(Company Name)
(Phone Number)
(Email)

(SUBJECT LINE)

_____

(OPENING PART)

_____

(BODY)

_____

(BOILERPLATE)

_____

_____

# # #

A release should not exceed one page, and the font must be easy to read. If you are trying to receive press for your business, a press release is vital. *Do you want to know a secret?* When people are submitting a press release to the media, be sure to do the following:

1) If your press release is in a Word document, adjust it to be a PDF, so it can be viewed by anyone.

2) Your email subject line should be the BOMB! Make the press outlets want to open your email and read it.

3) Attach your press release to the email, AND include it in the blank email form. In case the recipient cannot open the attachment, the press release will also be within the email. The recipient should be able to view your content, regardless.

4) After you have submitted a press release, follow up. Be prepared to hear "no" or "thank you for your submission; we will review it and get back with you." Reporters, writers, and editors receive hundreds of press releases – make sure yours stands out.

Submit a press release when you have an event, a new product release, a new hire, and changes in the company. Any major news that is relevant can go into a press release. Do not forget to double check your grammar and spelling!

Good sites to distribute your press release are:

- prnewswire.com

- 24-7pressrelease.com
- pr.com

A marketing kit is important to your business, so take the time to put it together correctly and update it. You should update key elements in your marketing kit about every six months.

Once you have a marketing kit, you will notice the increase in your business. It will become easier for you to convey your message, spread the word, and, most importantly, enhance your promotional efforts.

yourself for your business. There are many ways to increase SEO, and sometimes you have to try every one of these methods to get results.

SEO

What exactly does SEO mean for your business? SEO means attracting new clients and brand awareness. Think about when you search for a product or service online. For example, when I look for a plumber in the area, I will not go to the second and third page of Google to find one. I want the plumber who is located on the front page of Google and who has positive reviews. Many people believe that sites that are located on the lower end of search engine page ranking are less reputable. Since this is the game of the search engines, you must learn how to compete.

Here are five ways to increase SEO for free:

1) Become a headlining rock star: When you are crafting a headline, keep your audience in mind. A headline should captivate the reader's attention within the first five seconds. Put yourself in the reader's shoes. What kind of headline would make you click on the link to read the article?

2) Provide unique, clever, relevant and compelling content: Your content should be updated frequently to expedite the long climb of search engine ranking. The content should thrive on keywords.

3) Name each page within your website to be search engine friendly: Instead of having a page named *About Us*, go to the backend of that page and give it a unique name that helps search engine crawlers to pick up the page headers, tags and keywords on the page. For my media firm, Kindred Communications, externally, I named each page within the website its proper page name, but when I went to the backend (internally), I used keywords to explain the page like: branding| marketing| media| Houston| Texas. From there, I began to receive more visits on the entire website.

4) Pictures and videos are your friend...not your best friend: We all know that search engines love a good photo or video, but do not have your entire site filled with visual components. Strike a happy medium between the visual and content components contained in your website.

5) Tag...You're it!: Do not be afraid to tag with the best of them. You should be tagging everything on your website: posts, pictures, videos and pages. When tagging, use the best and most searched keywords. Tags allow search engines to find your page, which increases your chances that consumers will find your website, organically.

> **Bonus:** Hyper link where you can, but not too much. For example, if you write a post about the local coffee shop with which your business is partnering, be sure to link their site to the post. Search engines will increase your page ranks when you exchange links with other relevant websites. Encourage others to link to your website, as

well. SEO and page ranking depends heavily on links or mentions from other websites.

The key to SEO and page ranking efforts is to avoid overdoing any of your efforts, which can look like spam to search engines, and will not result in a high ranking. To gain views and improve your search rankings, determine what strategy works best for your business and continue to perfect these practices.

If you do decide to hire someone to help you improve SEO ranking and visibility, get references, a signed contract, current contact information, and a look at their online portfolio. There are so many people out claiming to be an "SEO Expert" who cannot produce results. Go with a well-known company. It may cost you more, but in the end, it will be worth the additional cost. If you see someone who has excelled in page views and search engine rankings, ask them how they achieved their success. Do not be afraid to hear *no* from people. You will be surprised about the relationships you can build with others who are eager to help new entrepreneurs. I constantly contact people who I admire and ask them questions. I may email someone in California or New York and just say *hi* and that I admire their work. Sometimes we chat about what we are doing and I am able to gain insight from a variety of people from diverse backgrounds. Often times, as business owners, we want to do everything on our own and not ask for help, but sometimes we need to ask for help and network, network, network!

You may have the greatest group of friends and colleagues, but there are many ways to expand yourself and your brand.

Chapter Six: Take Action

It is important to have a plan, but without a way to implement your plan, it is useless. I have seen business owners plan and prepare for focused marketing efforts, but they never take what they learned and push this information to the implementation phase. The following questionnaire is designed to help you organize your plan of action.

Why should you implement your plan quickly?

Your marketing efforts can become a faded memory. It is important to take action while the plan is fresh on your mind.

Should I do all my marketing efforts at the same time?

How do you eat an elephant? One piece at a time! You cannot manage all your marketing efforts at once. You must decide which is the most pressing and implement that one first. Which marketing effort is the most important to your business? How will it help your business?

Action Plan Questionnaire:

1) On a scale from 1 to 10, how good are you at the implementation process? One is poor and ten is excellent. (Circle one)

1   2   3   4   5   6   7   8   9   10

If you have circled anything below a 7, you need to analyze why you are not effective at implementation. If you do not analyze the source of the problem, you will continue to make the same mistake.

2) Why are you not effective at the implementation process?

_____

_____

_____

_____

3) If you believe you are effective at implementing your plan, list the reasons why.

_____

_____

_____

_____

4) If you think you are effective at implementing your plan, how can you improve to become great?

_____

_____

_____

_____

My implementation process is different than others, see below:

- **Plan:** Print your marketing plan and review it.
- **Review:** In reviewing your marketing plan, analyze what is required to execute your plan. Review your plan to see

what is realistic and what you might need to be altered or changed. This process should take about a week per subject to properly prepare to execute the plan effectively.

- **Strategize:** Strategize carefully, but do not stay on this step too long. I always believe in the saying, *"You think long, you think wrong."* When you are spending all your time strategizing and planning, you begin to second guess yourself. Move with confidence in your business.

- **Set your goal list:** What are your goals? Organize your goal list into weekly, monthly and yearly segments.

- **Prioritize:** Rank everything you do in a list from the most important to the least important.

- **Choose your area of focus:** Do not try to implement everything at once.

- **Attack**! Implement your marketing plan. You are going to make mistakes, which is part of learning to be an entrepreneur. Dive in and maximize your marketing efforts.

- **Practice makes perfect:** Develop a marketing habit. Since it takes 21 days to form a habit, try doing a 21-day marketing challenge. Create a marketing calendar to track your marketing efforts and how much you are spending on marketing every day. If you have a team of people working on your marketing, build a Google Calendar and Google Docs outlet, to avoid duplication of effort.

To begin your marketing efforts, use the form below.

Plan -Describe your overall plan in 1-2 sentences in the box to the right.	
Review -What are the pros and cons of your marketing efforts?	
Strategize - What is the first step to implement your plan?	
Goal List - What are your goals for the first month?	
Prioritize -What are the most and least important activities/items on your marketing list?	
Main Focus - What do you believe you should focus on first?	
Attack - Describe your plan of attack (implementation.) In 1-2 sentences.	
Practice - To make marketing a habit, what practices will you start off with?	

Chapter Seven: Freebies

To begin your marketing journey to grow your customer base, check out my top **five** free marketing ideas.

1) Host a giveaway: Hosting a giveaway will get people talking about your business. Yes, you are giving away some of your products or services, but in the end, a giveaway will help you gain new followers.

Name three potential giveaway ideas.

_____

_____

_____

_____

2) Webinars: By offering a webinar, you can become more of an expert in your field and a go-to source for clients. Help others in the industry, but do not give away all of your secrets. There's a thin line between being helpful and giving away too much. Decide what you are the best at in your industry and teach that expertise to others.

What are three webinar ideas you might have?

_____

_____

_____

_____

3) Create a monthly event: Get people talking about your business. When people have something to look forward to, they mark it on their calendars, tell friends and show up!

Putting on an event can be stressful, but the reward outweighs the stress. Putting on an event is another way to get your products and services in front of your customers without pressuring them to buy.

Name three events you could host to generate business?

_____

_____

_____

_____

What would you hope to gain from a monthly event?

_____

_____

_____

_____

When putting on an event, determine the date, time, location and type of event. After you decide these key elements, the rest will fall into place.

4) Go to a local apartment complex and host an on-the-go breakfast day: My favorite marketing event! I love a good breakfast on-the-go day. This breakfast event must be approved in advance by an apartment complex. Catch people coming out of their apartment gates and give them a free breakfast. When you give people the breakfast, you can also pass out company gear and collect email addresses for your e-newsletter. The breakfast does not need to be scrambled eggs and pancakes. Cereal bars, fruit and water bottles are more easily distributed. Two-to-three people from your team can successfully do this event.

Name three local apartment complexes that are located close to your target audience. Which ones would be appropriate for a breakfast day?

_____

_____

_____

_____

5) Learn more and increase your knowledge of marketing and communications by taking an online course at: lynda.com or udemy.com: If you need further help, it is a good idea to gain new knowledge and obtain additional skills in the field of marketing and communication, which can be difficult to acquire.

Do you want more free marketing and communication advice? Visit my company blog, *The Marketing Recipe* at kindredcommunications.wordpress.com.

Chapter Eight: Conclusion

If used properly, this book will serve as your personal guide to fulfill your dream of becoming a marketing rock star for your business. Thank you for trusting my guidance with your marketing efforts. Marketing your business is about creating habits that lead to success. Business success will not happen overnight but if you follow the steps in this book, you will build the necessary foundation to help your business grow, build awareness, and increase your audience.

Distinguishing your business from your competitors' businesses with your marketing efforts can be tricky and difficult. Sometimes you may feel like something has been done before and people are tired of it. You may be correct. That is why it is your responsibility to distinguish yourself and never give up. Be creative with everything you do and learn from your mistakes. Making mistakes is inevitable. Learn from them and keep trying.

Do not try to manage every marketing activity simultaneously. Implement your marketing plan one step at a time, and make your mark in your industry. Be patient with yourself and your business. Always enjoy the small strides you make, and plan for your future. Start today! Do not wait a month after reading this book. Get up, get out and market!

If you need further assistance, or simply do not feel like doing all of the marketing initiatives, my company, Kindred Communications, can help! Visit my company online and drop us an email to let us know how we may be able to help your business. We have worked with a variety of businesses from nonprofits to insurance companies. At Kindred Communications we treat you like family and help you invest in your future. Keep me posted on your marketing progress by contacting me on my website at kierstenkindred.com.

Plan, prepare and grow. Repeat.

"May your life be filled with joy, prosperity, and growth."

- Kiersten Kindred

About The Author

Founder and CEO of Kindred Communications, Kiersten Kindred, received her Bachelor of Arts from Sam Houston State University, where she graduated with magna cum laude honors with a major in Mass Communication and a minor in History. As a seasoned communications, marketing and media professional, she offers years of experience in small-business brand development to her readers.

Her company, Kindred Communications, is a full-service communications/media firm specializing in communications, marketing, entertainment, community engagement, consulting, career services and media relations for individuals to medium-sized businesses. Previously, she was the Publisher and Editor-in-Chief of the popular online magazine, A-List 180 Magazine – a weekly lifestyle, entertainment and culture online magazine.

Kiersten specializes in communications, media, marketing and defining brands. Keep up with her online at kierstenkindred.com.

Sources

1) Marketing. BusinessDictionary.com. Retrieved January 13, 2015, from BusinessDictionary.com website: http://www.businessdictionary.com/definition/marketing.html

2) Advertising. BusinessDictionary.com. Retrieved February 27, 2015, from BusinessDictionary.com website: http://www.businessdictionary.com/definition/advertising.html

3) Social Media Stats. Retrieved October 18, 2015, from Statista.com website: http://www.statista.com/statistics/265773/market-share-of-the-most-popular-social-media-websites-in-the-us/

4) Social Media For Your Business. Retrieved January 14, 2015, from Wix.com website: http://www.wix.com/blog/2014/03/social-networks-to-promote-your-business/

www.ingramcontent.com/pod-product-compliance
Lightning Source LLC
Chambersburg PA
CBHW070826180526
45168CB00002B/753